Empower Your Dreams

Let Go of Emotional Baggage So Affirmations Can Work for You!

By Janna Lee

Columbia Press

Printed in the United States of America

Library of Congress Control Number: 2020903633

ISBN: 978-0-9891131-5-1 (Paperback)

ISBN: 978-0-9891131-6-8 (Kindle eBook)

Book design by Susan L. Wells

*Dedicated to my grandmother, Marie;
my mother, Charmian; and my aunt, Joey.
They showed me by their examples how to live positively,
to always expect the best possible outcome,
and to often have it happen.*

I was and am so blessed!

Contents

Introduction 1
The Real Stuff—No Fluff

1. The Missing Step 3
   When a Dream Doesn't Come True
   The Missing Step
   Blocks to Manifesting Your Dreams
   A Road Trip

2. Formulas 9
   What We Do Naturally
   Formulas for Intentional Manifestation

3. Visualizing 15
   Visualizing Basics
   Imagining Basics

4. Affirming 23
   Creating your Affirmation
   Keep It Positive
   Frame It in the Present
   The Power of Allowing
   A Right

5. Feeling 31
   Feel the Appropriate Emotions
   Gratitude

6.   Possible Blocks 37
What Works
Three Levels of Awareness
Resistance

7.   Introduction to Clearing Methods 43
The Missing Step in Manifesting
Sowing on Good Ground

8.   Methods to Clear Your Blocks 47
Four Clearing Methods
Blow Bubbles
Stream the energy
A Stream flows by
Fill and Release

9.   Peeling the Onion 55
Not Once and Done
Approach from Different Angles

10.   Play It Forward 59

11.   Clearing Beyond Affirmations Program 65
Foundational Thoughts
Letting Go of Negative Chatter

12.   Tools to Support Manifestation 71
Make a Treasure Map
Design a Tableau
Wear or Carry Something Symbolic

13. **Actions to Support Your Dream** **77**
Preparing
Acting "As If"
Choose a Clearing Buddy

14. **Little Card Basics** **83**
What are the Little Cards?
The Little Cards Basic Format
Work with Attention and Lightness
The Little Cards Routine
Record Your Gains

15. **Supply** **91**
The Source of our Good
Characteristics
A Promise

16. **Unexpected Gifts** **95**

17. **Thoughts** **101**
It's Natural
Manifestation vs. Attraction
More Ways to Use Clearing Techniques
Affirmations for General Well- being

18. **My Story** **107**
Visualizing and Affirming
Emotional Healing
Energy Healing
Wrapping up

Thank You **115**

About the Author **117**

Empower Your Dreams

Introduction

The Real Stuff— No Fluff

Have you ever read a book full of stories about how other people used a teaching to improve their lives, and you felt empowered while reading? Then, disappointment came at the end of the book, because you realized that you were not given enough information to duplicate the improvements in your own life?

Well, *Empower Your Dreams* is just the opposite of that hypothetical book. It is basically a text on how to use clearing methods, along with visualizations and affirmations to make good changes happen for you. There is a story included here and there for emphasis, but mostly this is a how-to book.

So, who needs other people's accounts? The real stuff in this book will give you the tools you need to write your very own feel-good stories! ☀

All the best to you,

Janna Lee

Chapter One
The Missing Step

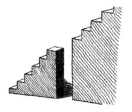

When a Dream Doesn't Come True

The Missing Step

Blocks to Manifesting Your Dreams

A Road Trip

When a Dream Doesn't Come True

O ften in the past when I would practice a program of visualizations and affirmations, my dream would not come true. Sometimes it would happen but more often it did not. And when I did not get the result I wanted, I would blame myself.

I would think that maybe I was not saying the affirmations often enough, or perhaps I was not visualizing with enough intensity. So I would try turning up the frequency and intensity of my practice. That did not work either.

I became frustrated. Why did what I focused on sometimes become reality and other times did not? So over the years, I continued studying and experimenting.

It finally dawned on me that my goal-setting was not happening in a vacuum. I had to look at the larger picture of what I believed in. It was then I realized that visualizations and affirmations alone were usually not enough. There was an additional and crucial step I had to take to allow my good to manifest.

The Missing Step

How can the good I desire come into my life when I hold beliefs that contradict its manifestation?

That is why visualizations and affirmations are usually not enough to make our dreams come true. We have to let go of our blocking negative beliefs and emotions that relate to what we desire in our lives, as well.

That is the missing step to manifest your dreams.

And you will be doing real work in letting go of beliefs and emotions that no longer serve you, but it is not hard work. Instead, it is easy to practice any of the four methods presented in Chapter Eight. All it takes is your commitment to keep releasing blocks that relate to what you want until you feel in a clear place. Then your dreams will have room to bloom.

Blocks to Manifesting

Yes, we can say, think, and write affirmations, see visualizations in our mind's eye, but that does not necessarily mean that what we desire will become reality.

It also does not necessarily mean that we are lacking in skill or concentration in using these manifestation tools. And finally, it does not mean that affirmations and visualizations do not work.

Instead, what it probably does mean is that we are experiencing some or all of these four conditions:

1. We do not want what we are picturing 100%. We have some unacknowledged ambivalence toward our dream
2. We do not feel that we deserve the good we are desiring
3. We have some negative opinions and/or emotions connected with our dream
4. And/or we have negative beliefs about the affirmation/ visualization process itself

So, how do you get beyond these four self-sabotaging states? You can do this by using any or all of the clearing techniques outlined in this book.

A Road Trip

Another Way to look at Self-Sabotaging Blocks

Suppose that you decide to take a vacation to a city near you. You research your destination and pick where you want to stay and eat, and what you want to see and do. You can just see it all in your mind's eye!

So, off you go, driving toward your vacation spot. After an hour, you run into a road block — one that does not show up on your GPS. However, you manage to find a detour and then you are on your way again. A little further along, you drive up to another blockade across the highway. When you stop, a nearby police officer comes to your car and advises you that a bridge has washed out over the river that you are approaching. Your delay here is much longer than the first detour, but eventually you find another bridge across the river.

You continue on, but soon you hear sirens and see flashing red and blue lights ahead. On this third stop there is a jackknifed truck blocking your way. Not only that, but there are hundreds of boxes that have spilled off the truck and litter the road.

After you wait awhile in a line of stopped cars and trucks, you decide to turn around and look for another way to get to your vacation destination.

That would be quite a road trip wouldn't it? But it is comparable to working toward making a dream come true without clearing mental and emotional blocks first. And in this fantasy trip you have an advantage of seeing or knowing what is getting in your way. Often, in the manifestation process, when you don't get to the destination you envision, you don't know why.

However, by using the clearing methods in this book, you can remove the blocks to realizing your dreams. Then you can write a story of your own journey without detours getting in the way. ☀

Chapter Two
Formulas

$$V + A = M$$

What We Do Naturally
Formulas for Intentional Manifestation

What We Do Naturally

When we strongly want something, what do we do? We are likely to think frequently about what we desire. If it is a physical object like a new outfit, we would probably daydream about having it and wearing it with our friends complimenting us.

If it is an event that we dream of like getting admitted to a college that we want to attend, we probably would see ourselves opening a letter of acceptance with great happiness. Or, if we want to be promoted at work, we most likely would visualize our boss telling us how happy he or she is with us and that we are moving to a new and better position in the business.

I believe that if we are easily experiencing this innate "seeing" process, we probably don't have a lot of interior baggage that works against our desires. There may be externals that oppose what we want that could still prevent our dream from realizing fully, but at least we would not have to clear away our internal opposition.

This natural way of mentally and emotionally going toward a goal often works. We all have done it. So let's realize that consciously using visualizations and affirmations is simply an extension of a natural process that is done in a thought-out and methodical way.

Formulas for Intentional Manifestion

Let's look at different programs of working to make our dreams come true.

In the purest and easiest scenario without mental or emotional blocks, an equation could be stated this way;

Visualizing + Affirming = Manifestation

Of course this formula does work, but often there will be negative beliefs that get in the way. Then an equation could say that manifestation does not happen:

Visualizing + Affirming ≠ Manifestation

However, using the releasing methods shared in this book, you could write the formula as:

Visualizing + Affirming + Clearing of Negative Beliefs = Manifestation.

Or, another way to write it would be:

Visualizing + Affirming – Negative Beliefs = Manifestation

However, there is an additional element to this equation. It is feeling — feeling that what you desire is already in reality. In my opinion, it is this feeling of already having what you want that creates the new reality. So the final equation could be:

Visualizing + Affirming + Clearing of Negative Beliefs = Feeling = Manifestation

We will look at the first two elements of the equations, visualizations and affirmations in *Empower Your Dreams,* although they have been covered quite a bit elsewhere. However, the main focus of this book is on the third part of the equations, the easy-to-use clearing techniques to help you remove blocking negative beliefs and emotions.

This is the real deal! If you hold strong beliefs that you will not be able to make your dreams come true through visualizations and affirmations, then you will not be able to do so.

Or, maybe you don't believe that you deserve good things in your life. Then your manifestation process would also be impeded or distorted.

It won't matter how many times you visualize something in your mind or how many times you make positive statements about your wished-for state or object. With strong negative beliefs contradicting your process, there will not be the out-picturing that you want.

The other thing to realize is that you don't have to be aware of what these negative beliefs are. They can be in your unconscious, perhaps created by what you experienced or heard as a child. That is why it is so important to keep using the clearing techniques even when you think you have let go of all your blocks. Just continue framing statements in a general way while practicing the clearing techniques so that you can release the ones which you are not aware of.

To help you let go of your emotional baggage, I also created the decks of Little Cards that focus on various goals you may have, such as for increased money flow, a loving relationship, or an event you want to happen in your life. They include positive statements to release a wide range of negative emotions to help speed up your process. ☀

Chapter Three

Visualizing

Visualizing Basics

Imagining Basics

Visualizing Basics

Tangible Goal

If you desire a solid object, then visualizing it is pretty straightforward. For instance if you want a specific new car, get a photo of it and then see it in your mind. Add the details, like color of interior and exterior. And see it in a setting that is appropriate for where you want it to manifest.

Also, to be sure to see the car in present time instead of the future, because it is now that is most powerful. See it in the future and that time may never arrive.

Get a strong still picture in your mind of your dream and then you can extend your visualization to an action one. You could see yourself enjoying driving your new car in your neighborhood. Or, you could visualize filling it up with gas or washing it. How about seeing yourself driving family members or friends to someplace special in the car of your dreams?

If you don't yet know exactly what car you want, then conduct some research. You can start by making a list of all the features that you desire in the car. Then you can focus your visualization on those features until you further narrow down what you are looking for.

Intangible Goal

A major challenge in making your interior movie comes when you want something intangible, like a romantic relationship. How do you visualize a new boyfriend or girlfriend?

The first answer is that you don't visualize someone you already know. It is not ethical to try to affect someone else's behavior with visualization. Therefore, if you like someone very much and want to be in a relationship with them yet know that they do not feel the same way, let it go. After all, everyone has free will given by our Creator, and it would not be in our best interest to try to mess with that.

Instead, a way to visualize experiencing a new romance is to focus on what you would be doing if you were already in a romantic relationship. For instance, you can see yourself getting ready to go out on a date you are looking forward to or sitting in a darkened theater watching a movie as you sit next to your new sweetheart.

As stated before, the goal is to feel that what you are wanting is already happening. If this works for you without seeing a specific boyfriend or girlfriend, then it can be effective.

However, most of the time I believe that when you desire something intangible, it is easier to depend on affirmations rather than visualizations to bring it into reality.

Imagining Basics

Using as Many Senses as Possible

One of the secrets of unlocking your dreams is to have the object or state that you are affirming seem as real as possible. The goal is to feel like you are already experiencing what you are visualizing. Adding as many senses to your process as possible can help make it feel real to you.

We have already looked at the sense of sight, since vision is the sense that we use the most. I have read that up to 80% of our information comes from what we see.

Hearing

Moving on to the sense of hearing, are there sounds that would be part of what you are wanting to manifest? For instance, if you are visualizing a new car, the sound of the engine revving up could apply. For more cash flow, you could hear the swish of bills moving from one hand to another as you count dollar bills. For romance, hear a song in your mind that you would like to listen to with a sweetheart. And another way to use sound is to imagine someone else making a comment that supports your affirmation.

For example, you could imagine someone saying, "How fortunate you are!" If you were affirming that you have an increased money flow, you could hear someone saying, "It looks like you have much more abundance in your life now!" Or, if you want a relationship, you could imagine someone saying, "You are so lucky in love! Look at what a wonderful boyfriend or girlfriend you have!"

Touch

As for touch, what would symbolize your affirmation becoming reality? For instance, if you want to get married, imagine wearing a wedding ring. You could even put a ring on your ring finger to see how it feels. Or, if affirming a new love in your life, you could imagine taking your boyfriend or girlfriend's arm as you are going on a date. For more cash flow, you could feel the money or a heavier wallet.

Or perhaps something else symbolizes having more money to you, like a piece of expensive and beautiful jewelry you could wear. Another possibility is to actually wear an inexpensive piece of costume jewelry that looks real. You could feel its weight on your apparel or touch it as you wear it.. This example would also work for using your sense of sight, as you could see yourself wearing it in your reflection in a mirror.

But, let's get back to the sense of touch. Another possibility is that you could feel like you are pushing a full cart of groceries with every possible kind of food that you like. Further, you could shut your eyes as you push your grocery cart in the supermarket and imagine it brimming over with all the goodies you like but don't buy now.

Smell

How about the sense of smell which is so primal? I am sure we have all experienced smelling something that instantly took us back to an earlier time. As an example, for me the smell of wet bark dust immediately takes me back to my childhood in Portland, Oregon, where rain often fell on bark dust that my mom used as mulch in the family garden.

Although the sense of smell is so powerful, I still find it hard to imagine a scent, and I assume you do too. Possibly the only way to use this sense is to have something provide the scent. Again, going back to focusing on a new car, I believe there are sprays that mimic the new car smell. How about spraying the area around you while you are visualizing?

Taste

Finally, there is the sense of taste. However, as with the sense of smell, I would find it hard to imagine a taste when I am working with affirmations and visualizations. The only way I can think to incorporate it into my imagining program is to actually eat something that relates to my dream. ☀

Empower Your Dreams

Chapter Four

Affirming

Creating your Affirmation

Keep It Positive

Frame it in the Present

The Power of Allowing

A Right

Empower Your Dreams

Creating Your Affirmation

Make your affirmation as simple and clear as possible. Here are some examples that address a wide range of dreams:

1. My life is filled with abundance now
2. Money lavishly flows to me now
3. I enjoy spending time with my wonderful boyfriend or girlfriend
4. I live in the home of my dreams
5. I love driving my new car
6. I allow myself to enjoy robust health and abundant energy now
7. I am so happy where I live
8. I allow myself to be positively recognized and promoted at work
9. I am writing my book smoothly and easily

In addition, always follow your affirmation with a declaration of gratitude or thankfulness.

Keep It Positive

It would be just as easy to make a list of things you don't want in your life as it is to make a list of things you do want. However, focusing on what you don't want will only help to attract those things to you.

Why? Because what we focus on is what we help manifest in our lives. I have heard that the mind does not hear "don't." Like we can tell a child, "Don't touch that hot stove burner!" However, the picture created in the child's mind is that of the hot burner, and the attraction to finding out about it may prove too strong for the child.

Instead, a positive redirect is more effective. We could say, "Stand back from the stove," or, "Come to me now."

I believe that the part of our minds that we address with affirmations is like the mind of a child and will focus on any image that we supply it. Therefore, it is important that we give our minds pictures of what we want.

Frame It in the Present

Affirm that you have whatever you desire in present time. For example, money flows to me now, or I am experiencing abundance now, or I have a wonderful sweetheart now.

Let's take a musical example with the lyrics of the "Hawaiian Wedding Song" by Al Hoffman and Dick Manning. The song goes, "This is the moment of sweet aloha." It doesn't say

"Tomorrow is the moment," or "Sweet aloha is coming any day now." No!

It says, "This is the moment," just as we should say in our affirmations.

After all, if we place our affirmation statement in the future, no matter how much time goes by, its manifestation will probably remain in the future.

The Power of Allowing

A typical response to wanting something to happen in your life might be to try to use your will to make it manifest, or to tighten your muscles and almost physically try to push it into reality. It is as if you really don't believe it is going to happen, but maybe if you make a lot of effort, it will.

Also please remember that when you are pushing for something, often there is a pushback. Without clearing your emotional baggage, a contradicting energy will probably come into play to block what you are picturing. What a mess! It is like a tug-of-war game in reverse.

Well, there is an easier way. Remove your blocking beliefs and emotions and then simply allow your dream to manifest. It sounds too easy doesn't it? But, it isn't. We just have to do our clearing work which isn't hard. Then we can step back and "allow" our dream to come true.

To remind us of the way it works, it is helpful to use the word, "allow" in an affirmation. An example is, "I allow myself to be in a healthy and fulfilling relationship." "Let" is a similar verb that can be used, like, "I let my trip to Maui come to me now."

You could also use the word, "OK," although I would probably combine it with "allow" or "let." An example would be, "It is OK for my trip to Paris to come to me now, and I allow it to come to me," or "I let it come to me now."

Other helpful words to use in crafting an affirmation are "smoothly," and "easily," as with this example, "Money flows to me now, smoothly and easily." Variations could be, "with ease," or "naturally." I suppose "simply" could be used as well. A useful phrase to use in an affirmation is, "I give permission," as in, "I give myself permission to get a raise at work." A shortened version would be, "I permit myself to…"

The beauty of using these words and phrases is that they can bring up more emotional baggage that you need to clear. For instance, you may feel that you don't deserve the good mentioned in the affirmations. Or you may think it should be difficult to get more money or a raise.

However, once you are conscious of your blocking beliefs or emotions, you can let them go using one of the methods in the book. And if your only clue of a block is that you feel uncomfortable using affirmations that describe an effortless process, it is still helpful. You can use the letting go techniques to release the discomfort which will move the negative energy too.

A Right

To think that what you are affirming should come to you as a right pushes the envelope beyond an "allowing" frame of mind. Using this approach may even cause you to have internal arguments with yourself. But, if you can get to a positive place with the idea, let's look at some phrasing that could work for you.

You could say, "I deserve," as in "I deserve to have a brand new red Corvette now." Personally, I have trouble using this phrase. One that is easier for me is, "I am worthy," as in I am worthy of having a brand new red Corvette now." Perhaps a more effective way to say that is, "I am worthy of having a new and beautiful car and I allow a brand new red corvette to come to me now."

You could also look at making your dream come true as something you deserve if you think of the process in terms of karma, like if you put good energy out in the Universe, you will get good energy back. An example, "I am a loving person and I deserve to be in a loving relationship." Another statement could be, "I work hard and am worthy of a good flow of money."

The benefit of using the "I deserve," and "I am worthy of" approach, is that these phrases can help you discover where you do not feeling deserving and worthy. Then you can use the clearing techniques outlined in this book to let these feelings go. ☀

Chapter Five

Feeling

Feel the Appropriate Emotions

Gratitude

Feel the Appropriate Emotions

*H*ow would you feel if what you were affirming became reality for you? Would you feel happy? Joyful? Loved? Would you feel cared for? Safe? Lucky? Fortunate?

In my experience, a major key to having my affirmations come true has been to feel the emotions I would feel if what I desired was already in reality.

This is big! Effectively using affirmations is not just about saying or thinking phrases. The manifestation recipe that works starts with visualizing and imagining what you desire, creating and using the positive statements about your dream, and then adding your feelings to make it happen.

And, anywhere in the process, I have found that the other major key is to use clearing techniques to remove negative beliefs that pertain to what you desire. After clearing, you can then get into feeling the emotions connected with achieving your dream.

Here is another way to look at the process, as though you were growing a garden:

1. Visualizing your dream happening in reality is like looking at photos of a beautiful, healthy plant in a seed catalog.
2. Saying and thinking the affirmations of what you want to appear is planting the seed in the soil.
3. Feeling emotions appropriate for the affirmation happening in reality is applying rich fertilizer to the planted seed.

4. Using the clearing techniques to remove blocks to your affirmation is removing weeds and rocks from the ground.

5. And happy process! Your seed in the ground grows into a glorious plant.

Gratitude

Gratitude gets a page all its own in the chapter on feelings. That is because I believe gratitude acts as a precursor to so many other emotions that can help in the dreams-coming-true process.

By expressing how grateful you are for something, I believe that you are automatically placing what you desire in present time, and that is what we want to do. I also find that when I am feeling grateful, I can also identify other positive feelings at the same time, like happiness, joy, or love connected to that for which I am grateful.

Here is an experiment:

1. Feel happy about something you are affirming. Are you able to do that?

2. OK, now feel grateful for receiving what you are affirming. Doesn't that automatically also make your feel happy?

Personally, I find that it is hard to create a feeling of happiness on its own, but I can have the feeling come to me when I express thankfulness. The goal is for you to get in a feeling place where you are already experiencing your good and are thankful for it.

And, in general, while working with visualizations and affirmations, it is helpful to have an "attitude of gratitude" for everything that is happening in your life. This is because the gratitude you focus on will tend to bring you more in your life for which to be thankful. ☀

Chapter Six
Possible Blocks

What Works

Three Levels of Awareness

Resistance

What Works

As mentioned previously, I discovered through using affirmations over the years that I usually have to do clearing and releasing first in order to have them work. The basic method with an affirmation is simply to say a statement of what you want to out-picture in reality. You then keep repeating and repeating it. Possibly you combine the affirmations with a visualization of the state or object you seek. However, often this process does not work to produce what you envision.

Usually this is because you have to remove the negative beliefs and emotions associated with ab affirmation first to make it effective. Until you take that step, it is like having an internal argument between your affirmation and some of your negative beliefs that cancels out creation of your dream.

So, how do you remove the contradicting beliefs? We know that just wanting them to go away is not enough.

I have learned that the first step is becoming aware that you are experiencing a level of physical or emotional tension regarding the goal you are affirming. This tension can occur on a continuum, with no awareness of why it is happening on one end, to very precise knowledge of what negative belief is creating the discomfort on the other end. No matter where the awareness is in this range, the next step is to use a clearing technique to let it go.

Three Levels of Awareness

To review, the most imprecise awareness of my personal negatives happens when I feel myself tensing up while saying an affirmation. That is my body telling me that the statement is not matching up with at least one thing I believe and the incongruity is creating physical stress. So, when I feel a tightening somewhere in my body, I know that it is time to let it go using one of the techniques outlined in the book.

It amazes me that when I release the physical tension connected with an affirmation, often my system also lets go of the belief or beliefs that caused it. After all, our mind-body connection is so strong.

A further clarity of my personal negatives happens when I have a negative feeling occur when I am stating an affirmation. Perhaps the statement seems to create a feeling of sadness or anger for me when I say it. Then I know that is what I have to clear.

One step further is to find the belief or beliefs that create the negative emotion or emotions. Clearing these from my energy system is the most precise way to achieve a clear space for my affirmations. For instance, while affirming that I have a wonderful boyfriend in my life, maybe I become aware that I have a belief that I am unattractive and also find that I believe I cannot have a boyfriend if that is the case. Therefore, I would release both those beliefs to clear the blockage.

To review, when you say an affirmation:

1. You may feel tense or constricted somewhere in your body, or

2. You may feel a negative emotion like sadness, anger or guilt, or

3. You may become aware of a negative belief that contradicts what you are stating in your affirmation.

This is the emotional baggage to let go of. We can do this by using one of the easy-to-use techniques in Chapter Eight.

Incidentally, I believe it is much easier to discover your blocks when saying affirmations as compared to when you are only visualizing what you desire. I find that when I have blocks to my visualizations, avoidance sets in and I become reluctant to continue doing them. It is just easier to stop. But with affirmations, somehow I want to start clearing and then carrying on with my positive statements.

Resistance

Resistance is a nonspecific block you may experience in doing this clearing work. Having awareness that resistance can interfere with your process of visualizing and affirming can help you continue to move forward.

I believe that our egos want everything to stay the same in our lives — perhaps in order for our life structure to continue on with minimum energy output, or maybe for us to feel safe. However, changes are promoted in your life when you use visualizations and affirmations. Adding clearing techniques to remove your blocks can alter your belief systems, and promote further change. All this can threaten your ego's status quo, and resistance can pop up.

It seems like our ego should not resist changes that could improve our lives. However, even when what we are seeking is in our best interest, and I hope that applies to everything we are trying to have happen, resistance can occur. For instance, I am a writer. I like to write and it is rewarding on many levels for me to do so, but I can experience resistance in the form of wanting to procrastinate at any time.

In this state, I can find innumerable excuses not to sit down at the computer keyboard, even though I know that I would feel happy and fulfilled if I did start writing. I could even create another article or book which could be financially rewarding, but when I am experiencing resistance, I don't want to write.

You could experience resistance as well, using the Little Cards to increase your money flow, or find a sweetheart, or experience more success. I would expect that at some time in the process, you will want to stop, downplay your gains, or just want to put the cards aside for no particular reason you are aware of.

Knowing that you can expect resistance is half the battle to overcome it. The other half is to clear the resistance with the same energy techniques presented in Chapter Eight for releasing negative emotions and beliefs. ☀

Chapter Seven

Introduction to Clearing Methods

The Missing Step in Manifesting

Sowing On Good Ground

The Missing Step in Manifesting

L etting go of your emotional baggage gives you a clear place to manifest what you desire. Just think of your brain as a powerful computer that is always working. It records all that happens to you, including data from all of your senses, plus all that you think and feel. Then your brain is ready to replay the appropriate tapes back to you when you are presented with a situation that feels similar to something that has happened to you before.

For instance, say that you want to find a new and fulfilling job that uses your talents. Start affirming this and your memory will play back at least the most obvious tapes you have recorded about work. I would guess that there are probably as many negative memories and beliefs that would come up as positive ones. Then add in emotions you felt when you were in unhappy job situations, and that adds up to quite a bit of feedback coming your way.

So, what can you do? Practice the missing step of letting go of emotional baggage that weighs down your program! Four clearing methods of letting go are detailed in the next chapter.

Just think how fortunate we are. Previously the only choice available to attempt this clearing was to go into lengthy counseling or psychotherapy. (And, yes, I have done that in the past and highly recommend it if you think you need it.) However, the clearing techniques have worked for me to get to a place where some of my dreams have come true.

Another way to visualize the process is that we are clearing away our personal negatives to achieve the fertile ground that we need to grow our visualization and affirmations into reality.

I believe the book of Matthew, Chapter 13, in the Bible describes the work we are doing. This is from the King James Version.

Sowing on Good Ground

Matthew, Chapter 13
Verses 3–9
King James Bible

3 And he (Jesus) spake many things unto them in parables, saying, behold, a sower went forth to sow,

4 And when he sowed, some seeds fell by the way side, and the fowls came and devoured them up;

5 Some fell upon stony places, where they had not much earth: and forthwith they sprung up, because they had no deepness of earth;

6 And when the sun was up, they were scorched; and because they had not root, they withered away.

7 And some fell among thorns; and the thorns sprung up, and choked them;

8 But other fell into good ground, and brought forth fruit, some an hundredfold, some sixtyfold, and some thirtyfold.

9 Who hath ears to hear, let him hear. ☀

Chapter Eight

Methods to Clear Your Blocks

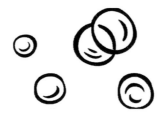

Four Clearing Methods

Blow Bubbles

Stream the Energy

A Stream flows By

Fill and Release

Four Clearing Methods

Four energy techniques to clear and release your blocks to manifestation are:

1. Blow Bubbles
2. Stream the Energy
3. A Stream Flows By
4. Fill and Release

Don't let the picturesque names fool you into thinking these ways to release negative thoughts, beliefs and emotions are lightweight. They are not. Even though they are easy to use, they do work.

All of the techniques start with you saying or writing an affirmation. If you don't experience any contradiction to what you are affirming, you simply proceed on in your practice. However, often you will experience internal pushback to the statement, and that is when you use one of the clearing methods.

You could feel the pushback as tension somewhere in your body. Or perhaps it is in the form of an uncomfortable emotion like anger. Or, you might even be aware of a conflicting statement going through your head. Like if you are affirming, "More money flows into my life now," you might become aware of an answering statement saying, "Fat chance more money is coming to me!"

Whatever the form of contradiction to your affirmation, next ask yourself: "Am I ready to let go of this energy? If the answer is, "Yes," you can say something like, "I choose to release this energy now." Then begin using one of the techniques until it feels like all the negative energy is moved from your energy field. In my experience, it usually takes me from one minute to a few minutes.

Then, send yourself love and light. You can see yourself filled with light in your imagination and possibly feel warmth or even love in the process. You could add statements of self praise as well. Since nature abhors a vacuum, it is good to replace the energy you have moved.

Please remember to be gentle with yourself while using any of the clearing methods. You do not need force to move the energy, just have the intent to. You are simply letting it leave — not using your will to make it go. Also, please stay nonjudgmental about the thoughts, beliefs and emotions you are releasing. While you are finding that they no longer serve you, they must have helped you live your life in some way at an earlier time.

Method 1
Blow Bubbles

To use Method 1, visualize that you are blowing your unwanted negative thoughts, beliefs and emotions into bubbles.

Since you are using your mouth to blow the energy and can't speak, you may find it helpful to think statements like, "I let the energy go. It no longer serves me. The energy moves easily. I release it to the Universe."

Visualize filling one bubble after another with the negative energy you are releasing from your system. As the bubbles fill, they expand and rise into the air. They float away high above you and pop.

The energy is then absorbed by the Universe. It is purified and turned into light.

When you feel that you are finished with letting go of the energy, send yourself self-approval, and love and light from our Creator.

Method 2
Stream the Energy

With Method 2, you visualize the negative thoughts, beliefs and emotions as energy leaving your body, usually from the front, but sometimes from the back. Frequently it feels like the energy departs from your head, chest or abdomen, but it could be from any area of your body.

First, sense from where the uncomfortable energy wants to leave, and secondly state that you are ready to let it go. Then you can see or sense the energy streaming out of your energy system.

If may be helpful to make hand motions as though helping the energy move out. You can also state to yourself that you are streaming the energy — that it is leaving your body and energy field. You can say something like, "I see the energy moving out," or "I let it go." Or another statement could be, "The energy streams out easily. It takes no effort. It just moves out into the atmosphere and turns into light."

If it is helpful to you, visualize the energy as a color or colors.

Continue with the process until you feel that you have cleared most of the energy. That time period could be from about a minute to a few minutes.

As a reminder, when you are finished, stream the Creator's love and light into your body or energy field. Also you can praise yourself for taking good personal care and freeing yourself of potential blocks to self-expression and well-being.

Method 3
A Stream Flows By

Thanks to my Aunt Joey for sharing Method 3 with me. I like it because it is easy to use and focuses on water which is symbolic of emotions.

Imagine that you are standing by a stream that originates somewhere in front of you and flows past you. It can run on either side of you, although personally, I prefer the left side. Or, you could imagine streams flowing on both sides of you.

After saying an affirmation, you become aware of a physical tightening or negative emotion or belief in your system. You visualize it as energy inside you. Then, with your hands, imagine that you take some of the energy from your body — possibly from your chest, stomach, abdomen, mouth or legs, depending on where it feels appropriate.

Drop the energy into the stream or streams and see it float away behind you. Keep visualizing that you are gathering the energy in your hands and releasing it into the stream. Do this as long as you feel that some of the negative energy remains in your system.

Like with Method 1, you may find it helpful to affirm that you are releasing the energy from your body to be cleansed by the universe. It leaves your system easily. You are neutral towards the energy; it is just time for it to move on.

When you feel you have finished letting go, send yourself approval for doing this work, and let the Creator's love and light fill your body.

Method 4
Fill and Release

Clearing Method 4 is one of the easiest techniques to use.

Simply hold your hands open horizontally at waist height. Then imagine you are filling up your hands with your unwanted energy of negative beliefs and emotions. When your hands feel full, make a releasing gesture with them. To do this, I close my hands and then open them vigorously.

See or feel the energy that you are letting go of dissipating smoothly into the atmosphere and going back to Source. Continue the technique until you feel that this energy has moved out of your system.

Then send yourself self-approval until you can feel it. You could also see love and light coming to you from the Universe. ☀

Chapter Ten
Play It Forward

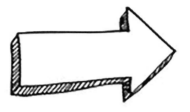

Play It Forward

I t can be beneficial to build an energy support structure for what you want to have happen. That is a fancy way of saying that in addition to visualizing and affirming what you want to achieve, also play it forward to see yourself happily and confidently enjoying that something after you get it.

For instance, if you want a promotion at work, visualize yourself in the role you want. Maybe it would be a management or higher management position that you are wanting. See yourself doing your work and directing your staff smoothly and easily and feeling good about it.

If you have trouble visualizing working in your new position or whatever you want, try creating affirmations about it. That is because I have found that when I have a hard time seeing something happen, it is easier to make statements about it. This usually happens when I am experiencing blocks, and the affirmations will probably bring up some of the negative beliefs and emotions that I have about your goal. Then you can let the blocks go with one of the clearing techniques outlined in *Empower Your Dreams.*

Playing it forward on what you are visualizing and affirming can be helpful to you in two ways. One outcome is that you may decide you do not want the object of your focus after all. Think of teenagers today who want to be influencers on the internet. Probably all they can think of is all the followers they would have and how popular they would feel. However, I'll bet they are not thinking about the hard work required of making videos and posts, or the lack of privacy they would have.

The other playing-it-forward outcome you could have is becoming aware of fears, negative feelings and other blocks that stand in the way of your manifestation. Assuming that you still want what you have been dreaming of, you can then release them.

Here is a personal example of when I intensely wanted something but did not considered what would happen if I got it. I was a high school senior in Portland, Oregon and very much wanted to be chosen Rose Princess by the students. It was something that girls growing up in Portland were very aware of, especially if their family took them to see the Rose Festival Parade.

As Princess, I would have represented my school in the Rose Parade in June and gotten to ride on the Rose Court float. Being Princess was not something that I worked on consciously; I just thought it would be wonderful to be chosen. Looking back, I guess that I unconsciously focused on being announced as Princess in my high school assembly after a vote of the students.

What happened is that I sailed comfortably through an elimination process where six of us senior girls were chosen to be on our school's court. But after that, I started feeling anxious leading up to the assembly that featured each of us giving a speech to the student body before the voting for Princess occurred.

I did not know then how to address my fears and release them like I do now. So I tried to ignore my anxiety and it manifested as a physical problem instead. The roof of my mouth became inflamed after I ate some Fritos! (That had never happened to me before and has not happened since.) This condition made it harder for me to give my speech because the puffy top of my mouth made it a challenge to enunciate clearly, the result being that I sounded like I had a lisp.

I think I could have saved myself from that whole speech problem if I had known what is in this book. Beyond that, I don't know what the outcome would have been nor does it matter. A very deserving classmate was announced as Princess, and while I was sorry it was not me, I was also relieved. It was a lesson in learning that I was not going to get everything I wanted, and this goes for the affirmation and visualization process too. Higher Power or the Universe is always at work, and maybe the best and highest good for all concerned means that we don't always reach our goal, especially if we are competing with others for it.

However, the point here is that if I had done the clearing of my anxiety and fears, I would have been much more comfortable during the selection process, and been able to feel that I had done my best.

This is only an example of showing that using clearing techniques can be beneficial. And, yes, maybe it is time for me to clear away whatever still bothers me about this and realize I did the best I could at the time.

So, I say, "Thank you Universe! There always continues to be growth opportunities in my life to work with." ☀

Chapter Eleven

Clearing Beyond Your Affirmations Program

Foundational Thoughts

Letting Go of Negative Chatter

Foundational Thoughts

A s babies and kids, we all created internal statements to explain what we were experiencing. If our environment was responsive to our needs most of the time, we created favorable statements. And if we heard positive comments about ourselves from those around us, especially our parents and caregivers, we probably decided that we were good and worthy.

On the other hand, if our parents and the folks around us were not responsive when we were hungry and crying, we could have decided that we were not worthy of being cared for. We could have also decided that the world was a hard place to have our needs met.

I call these foundational thoughts — internal statements derived from both our early experiences and early feedback from others. These provide a basis for what we expect later in life. They can repeat over and over in our heads, or we may only be aware of the emotions derived from them, like having general feelings of pessimism or optimism, of despair or hope. We are probably more fortunate if we are conscious of our recurring internal statements. When we know what they say, we can decide which are beneficial to us and which are not.

Let's think of examples of foundational thoughts. Positive ones from childhood could be as common as, "I am a good boy," or "I am a good girl," or "I am smart," or "I am a helper." Some examples of negative thoughts could be, I am a bad girl," or "I am a bad boy." Other examples could be, "I am too noisy," or "I am clumsy," or "I am stupid."

When working with affirmations, probably most of our

foundational positive thoughts support them. Where we hit a head wind is when foundational negative and self-critical statements come up to contradict what we are affirming.

It is important to make an effort to become aware of any of these repetitive self-critical statements that parade through our minds. This is because they can sabotage any manifestation program that we are practicing, besides making our lives miserable. And they may stay dormant if our lives happen to mirror these self-statements, but if you are practicing a program of self improvement, they can start to replay in your mind.

If you are not aware of what these statements are, you can work backwards from an uncomfortable feeling, like one off pessimism or sadness, to see if you can identify what you have told yourself to make you feel that way. If that does not work, you can still use the clearing methods to release the negative feelings and that will probably remove the self-sabotaging beliefs as well.

And if you know what the foundational negative thoughts are it is even easier to clear them using any of the methods described earlier in the book. After that, if the thoughts continue, you can create an opposite affirmation. For instance, if a foundational thought says that, "My needs will not be met," you could say, "My needs are abundantly met. I am so grateful."

Further, if a foundational negative or self-critical thought comes up, you can say, "Cancel." Then say an affirmation that is the opposite of the negative though. Another way to become aware of these thoughts is to wear a rubber band around your wrist. When one of the negatives comes to mind, snap the rubber band, followed by the opposite affirmation.

As you continue with your clearing, you will probably find that you no longer feel sadness, guilt, anger, jealousy, or other negative feelings when working your visualization and affirmation program. Then you will know that you have let go of your unhealthy self-statements through releasing the emotions connected with them.

No one said that it is easy to make positive changes in your life, but it is possible. That is why I wrote this book — to encourage you to "keep on keepin' on." My experience is that wondrous change can and does happen, sometimes sooner and sometimes later. We just have to persevere.

Letting Go of Negative Chatter, Both Internal and External

Being on an intensified path toward positive change in my life, I now often notice when I am thinking critical or negative thoughts or making critical comments about something or someone. Probably that is because the contrast is highlighted between the positive affirmations and remaining negativity in my thoughts and actions.

I think that we all have a whole range of automatic responses and thoughts to situations we frequently encounter. For instance, I can get highly impatient when I am driving and traffic is slow. Then a litany of critical comments can begin circling in my head. I can also get very critical of people cutting in front of me or tailgating me.

Now I am realizing that I do not have to respond in these habitually critical ways when I am driving. I could say to myself, "Oh it is just traffic. I will still get to where I am going." I can just relax and listen to music or a recorded book. I could even take the remediation further and imagine that someone I really like to be with is sitting in the passenger seat. Then, I would want the drive to last as long as possible!

Also, negative chatter about others can be so tempting. Gossiping can make us momentarily feel superior to whomever we are talking about, but what are the negative effects to us? Do we really want a reputation for saying bad things about others? And doesn't that then invite others to say bad things about us?

I am bringing up general negative thinking and speaking because I think they can drag down our program of visualizing and affirming. I do not have any proof of that, but it does make sense to me. It feels to me like this internal and external chatter can make it harder to switch back to the positive place I need to be to carry on with making my dreams come true. ☀

Chapter Twelve

Tools to Support Manifestation

Make a Treasure Map

Design a Tableau

Wear or Carry Something Symbolic

Make a Treasure Map

Another way to support a dream-to-reality goal is to put together images on poster board that symbolize what you desire. You can use your own photos and drawings or get images from the internet or magazines. This visualization tool is called a "treasure map" or "vision board," and Unity Church has been teaching how to make them for a long time. In fact, you can purchase a booklet about treasure mapping from Unity.org.

You could also make an electronic version of a treasure map on PowerPoint, again using images from your own photos or from free online stock photos. You could even create a simple repeating loop of these images to watch when you have a spare minute.

Design a Tableau

A tableau is what I call an arrangement or grouping of items that symbolize what I am affirming. Personally, I have enjoyed using this manifestation tool.

How to create a tableau:
1. Pick a flat surface around 2 feet by 3 feet, like on a table or desk. You could even pick a space in a drawer if surface space is limited or if you want privacy.

2 .Next, it is desirable to place a piece of heavy paper or poster board on the surface to act as a base to visually connect all the objects together.

3. Then put three or four items on the paper that are related to what you are visualizing and affirming. Arrange the objects in a way that makes sense to you and is in a harmonious arrangement so that you will enjoy looking at it.

For instance, if you are making a tableau to increase your money flow, you could place a piece of jewelry, a pile of paper money, a photo of a new car, or whatever else would symbolize having more money coming your way. You could even use a cornucopia shaped item from a craft store in the tableau, since cornucopias themselves are symbolic of abundance. Then you could arrange your money symbols to spill out of this horn of plenty.

For affirmations to bring a new love into your life, you could place a rose, either artificial or real, a greeting card showing two lovers on it, perhaps replicas of tickets to a play you would like to see with a new sweetheart, or a photo of a restaurant you would like to go on a date.

As you can gather, the tableau arrangements are only limited by your creativity.

Wear or Carry Something Symbolic

If you are affirming abundance in your life, you could carry one hundred dollar bills or larger denominations in your wallet. If you are affirming having a new love, you could put a photo in your wallet of someone you think is attractive.

If you are affirming a trip to Hawaii, how about on the wearing on the weekend, what you would wear if you were on the islands?

Jewelry is always a good symbol. For instance, a woman could wear a ring similar to what she would like to receive from a boyfriend. Or, if you would like flying lessons, you could wear an aviator's watch with all the dials.

I think wearing something symbolic of what you desire is powerful because when you do that, two senses are engaged — sight and feeling. As an example, wearing a ring on a finger or a watch on your wrist enables you to see the symbolic object and also receive the kinesthetic sense of it. What you might find is that the sense of feeling delivers a stronger message because it is more unconscious and subliminal. ☀

Chapter Thirteen

Actions to Support Your Dream

Preparing

Acting "As If"

Choose a Clearing Buddy

Empower Your Dreams

Preparing

I f you know that something you want to have happen is coming soon, don't you prepare for it?

Then, of course, you should also prepare for something that you are visualizing, affirming, and clearing for.

It is pretty simple, isn't it? If you think your good is going to be in your life soon, then it is good to be ready for it.

Acting "As If"

Acting "as if" could be called a taking part in a dress rehearsal for actually experiencing what you dream of. This is very powerful because if you act a certain way, the feelings associated with your actions follow. It will help you to feel like your dream has come true just as much or maybe more than visualizing and affirming it.

And I do believe that feeling like the Universe has already manifest your dream is the final step to having it happen.

So, ask yourself, "How would I act if my dream came true?"

Let's take the example of having more money or abundance in your life. For instance, we know through the ages that tithing, or giving 10% of your income to your place of worship, has been encouraged and spoken of as a way to have increased money come back to you. Obviously, there is a large degree of faith that one must have in order to tithe. A person would be acting on the belief that the income would be continuing and that their remaining income would be sufficient after the gift of 10%.

I am not advocating tithing in this book, but mentioning it as a profound way of acting "as if" that has been practiced for thousands of years.

So, how would you act if your dream were in reality?

In regard to abundance, you would probably act in a confident manner, knowing that you have abundance and/or money to supply your needs and the needs of the ones you love. And, that confidence alone can act like a magnet to draw good things to you.

Or, say it is a sweetheart for which you are affirming. If you were already in a relationship, would you act differently? Would you be more attentive to your personal grooming and dress more attractively? Would you go out more to social or sporting events and be more outgoing? Those are some of the questions to ask, and I am sure that you can think of more.

Choose a Clearing Buddy

Having a partner to work with can be helpful in your program of clearing away old negative beliefs and emotions. You could meet in person or talk on the phone regularly to share any blocks that have come up for your affirmations. You could then use any of your clearing methods with your clearing buddy as a witness. In turn, you could support them as they practice clearing their blocks.

Of course you can do this effectively by yourself, but working with someone else seems to make the techniques even more powerful. Plus it is nice to have a witness to what you are doing, and to be of service to someone who is working to better their life. ☀

Empower Your Dreams

Chapter Fourteen
Little Card Basics

What are Little Cards?

The Little Cards Basic Format

Work with Attention and Lightness

The Little Cards Routine

Record Your Gains

What Are Little Cards?

L ittle Cards are decks of cards with affirmations on them which I created to help with the manifestation of specific goals.

They are the size of business cards, measuring 2 inches by 3-1/2 inches. There are 28 basic cards per deck so that you can focus on one affirmation per day for four weeks. Or you could go through all the cards every day. Choose whatever works best for you.

In addition, there are a varying number of bonus cards per deck to help you in your process.

I originally created them for my own use in order to make my affirmations program easier. In addition to positive statements, the decks include cards expressing gratitude and cards addressing blocks in a positive way that may need clearing.

Now I want to share the Little Cards with you as well. So far, there are decks affirming increased money flow and finding your love. More will be created soon.

The Little Cards Basic Format

A deck of Little Cards starts out with a card stating the theme of the deck. It will affirm that some good is in your life like money, abundance, a sweetheart, success, a job or something else you desire.

Following cards in a deck express gratitude or happiness various ways. Your different senses will also be called out throughout the deck, such as for hearing, "I hear someone say that I am so fortunate." For the kinesthetic sense, you could say, "I feel my sweetheart holding my arm," or "I feel the boarding pass in my hand as I get ready to board the plane."

A very important part of any deck will be statements of releasing possible blocks to your main affirmation. Listing the various kinds of blocks is done as a prompt to help you in discovering your own personal negatives, because your emotional baggage may not be in your conscious awareness. Also affirming that you are releasing them can be helpful on its own. So these cards may seem simple on the surface, but they are meant to inspire deep clearing work on your part.

Why are the Little Cards little? As my petite mother used to say, "Good things come in small packages," and that is the case with these cards. They are small because that makes them easy to carry in a pocket or bag. They are business-card-size so they can be displayed in a business card display holder or carried in a business card case. Also, you can look at them in public and others will just suppose that you are looking through a collection of business cards.

Work with Attention and Lightness

The goal of using the cards is to provide help to you in allowing your good to manifest. It is really important for you to know that the goal is NOT to force yourself to believe in what you are affirming — it is to ALLOW your good to come to you!

I know that when I started using affirmations many years ago, I would tense myself up and will myself to believe. I was putting a lot of effort into creating something good that I wanted in my life. Occasionally what I was affirming would appear and I would be so happy! However, more often, there would not be the manifestation I desired. Then I would criticize myself for somehow not using the statements in the right way or not believing in them enough.

Thank goodness the Little Cards are different. Using them takes the pressure off of you to do it "right." All you are doing is getting out of the way and letting your good come to you. Of course, a major part of getting out of the way is for you to clear out old beliefs and negative emotions that no longer serve you. But the clearing process is not hard to do.

So, use the cards with attention and lightness! It is so much easier than working with tension and besides, it is enjoyable.

The Little Cards Routine

Go through the cards at least once a day, reading them or saying the affirmations out loud. You can also alternate the way you say the affirmations. You can say them the first time the way they are written. Then, the second time, when you say, "I," add your name after. For example, I would say, "I, Janna…" The third time, repeat the affirmation as though you were speaking of someone else, using your name. For instance, I would say, "Janna has increased money flow coming to her now. She is so thankful!"

Another way to add power to the statements is to combine

saying them with physical movement. You can get a beat going and say them while walking, cycling, or dancing.

Or, how about singing your affirmations? Varying how you input them makes the statements seem new and keeps them interesting.

To further impress the affirmations on your mind, you can display a different card every day in a business card holder. You could also use additional card holders to display cards in various rooms of your home. Or you can take the Little Cards with you in a card case and read the affirmations while at lunch or coffee.

Record Your Gains

Part of the Little Cards program is writing down your gains every 24-hour period, related to what you are affirming.

For instance, if you are calling for more money flow in your life and unexpected money comes to you — write it down.

Or, if you are affirming that you have a new love in your life and you meet or go out with someone you are interested in — write it down. How about if you are affirming that you are taking a trip to Bali — write down daily any steps you are taking to make the journey.

If you want, you could also have pages devoted to any changes in your attitudes or behaviors that could contribute to the manifestation of your dreams.

So, get yourself a small notebook to use with each deck of Little Cards. Recording your gains will make them seem more real to you and help you to realize that you are making progress toward your goal.

After all, haven't you heard at one time another, someone say that something (fill in the blank) must be true, because they read it in a paper or on the internet? It is the same with your unconscious mind which works with your conscious mind to make a manifestation. Reading about your gains helps that childlike part of your mind get onboard with your program.

Also, writing down your gains is good discipline and keeps you on track using the cards. Due to resistance, most of us will be tempted to stop our program of visualizing, affirming and clearing at some point. That is because as a gain fades into history, it becomes easier to dismiss it, like it was not a big deal after all, when it really was. But, if we record a gain when we are still excited and amazed, it will be harder for us to downplay it later. ☀

Chapter Fifteen

Supply

The Source of our Good

Characteristics

A Promise

Empower Your Dreams

The Source of Our Good

I t is easy to think that the source of our money or abundance is our job, or that the source of love for us is our family, friends, or significant other. And, yes, our work or the people in our life are channels of these good things that come to us, but not the source.

In the *Empower Your Dreams* teaching, the source of our good is our Creator, or the Universe, or God, or our Higher Power — whatever you choose to call what is greater than ourselves. When we realize this, we become much more open to receiving from many channels, instead of just the customary ones.

Characteristics

Since our supply or good comes from Higher Power or our Creator, it makes sense that it would mirror the qualities of that source.

What would some of these qualities be? One that comes to mind is that my good would be unlimited or limitless. It would be abundant too. How about describing it as infinite?

All of these adjectives or variations of them can be used when you craft affirmations.

Here are some examples: "I draw from the well of unlimited supply," or, "my Higher Power surrounds me with lavish abundance."

Because of the source of our good, I try to remember when I am saying an affirmation, to close it with, "Please Higher Power, this or better." Sometimes we don't think big enough, and this should open our minds to the possibility of a larger manifestation.

A Promise

As a child in Sunday School, I especially loved two verses in Chapter 7 of the Book of Matthew in the Bible. I believe today that they are relevant to us in when we want a better life for ourselves using the tools in this book.

Here are the verses:

Matthew, Chapter 7
Verses 7 and 8
King James Bible

7 Ask, and it shall be given you; seek, and ye shall find; knock, and it shall be opened unto you:

8 For every one that asketh receiveth; and he that seeketh findeth; and to him that knocketh it shall be opened. ☀

Chapter Sixteen

Unexpected Gifts

Unexpected Gifts

I have been pleased to receive unexpected benefits when I have been in the process of affirming, visualizing and clearing for a desired outcome.

For example, when focusing on abundance, I have become much more aware of the plenty that is already in my life. Also, my definition of abundance seems to enlarge every time I continue on an affirmation path for it. It grows to include relationships I enjoy — the people whom I love or like and who love or like me. Also added is what I like about my home and larger environment, pets in my life, projects I am immersed in, and even books I am reading.

And being aware of all the richness I already experience leads me to feel more gratitude and peace. You could say that my definition of abundance becomes more spiritual. More abundance may become available to me as well, but I end up experiencing the whole process as enriching.

Visualizing and affirming that I will receive an increased money flow is looking for a more tangible result. While more abundance can mean all sorts of things, increased money flow means just that — more monetary units or dollars! However, I still have found that the scope of my measuring and creating this flow widens in the process. Instead of waiting for a pile of money to fall in my lap without any effort on my part, I gained a heightened awareness of money-making and money-saving opportunities that were already in my life.

With that awareness, I have pursued those possibilities and added to my money flow. I believe that what the manifestation process gave me was a willingness to act. I had known of most of the earning and saving opportunities prior to my affirming, visualizing and clearing, but had chosen not to do anything about them. I had told myself that what I was looking at was not important enough to pursue, or entailed too big a learning curve for me to make it worthwhile.

My becoming aware that I already had power to implement my desired outcome of more abundance and/or money before I even started my program reminds me of a joke you have probably heard, but it is worth repeating:

Joe is standing on the roof of his house in great distress, looking at chaotic flood waters lapping at his second story. He desperately prays to God to rescue him. A little later, two men row a boat up to him and hold out their hands to help him into their craft. Joe declines their offer. In another few hours, a helicopter zooms up and hovers over his house. A voice from a loudspeaker asks if he would like to be rescued, and he says, "No."

The water keeps rising and later another man paddles a rubber raft up to Joe. "I am here to rescue you," he says. Reluctantly, Joe manages to get in the raft. Joe says, "Thank you, but I am so disappointed! I prayed to God to rescue me, and I didn't hear an answer, so I guess I will have to go with you."

Of course, the actions of this imagined Joe are ridiculous. However, this joke reminds me to look at my expectations of how my good will come to me when I am looking for a desired outcome. Perhaps my good does not come to me to way I want it to or think it should. However, I have to be open to other ways to receive. It is all good. ☀

Chapter Seventeen

Thoughts

It's Natural

Manifestation vs. Attraction

More Ways to Use Clearing Techniques

Affirmations for General Well-being

It's Natural

The visualization-affirmation process is a natural one — not some hocus pocus kind of magic. Just think what you did when you intensely wanted something before reading this book. I will predict that you thought often about the object or state that you desired. You would have been picturing it in your mind if it was a material object, or seeing yourself acting appropriately in your imagination as if it was a happening like finding a new love. You also might have had some kind of repetitive statement you thought about or even said out loud like, "I can just see myself driving my new car," or, "My boss is going to promote me to supervisor; I just know it."

You use the same process with visualizations and affirmations, but in a more thorough way. I think consciously visualizing and saying affirmations heightens your focus on what you are doing. Instead of daydreaming of what we want in a desultory way, you visualize and speak your affirmations with more concentration.

But that does not make the manifesting process magic or supernatural. What it does mean is that in the process, you become clear about what you desire and craft your visualizations and affirmations with care. Then you embark on a "seeing and saying" program that hopefully leads you to feeling that you already have what you want. And, of course, you use the often neglected step of clearing negative beliefs in order to actualize your dreams.

So, magic — no! But effort and focus — yes!

The Law of Manifestation
vs.
The Law of Attraction

I prefer to say that the practice of using visualizations, affirmations and clearing is part of the Law of Manifestation.

Why? Because by manifesting, I am bringing some good into reality that is already a part of me in some way. It is moving from the inside to the outside.

I look at the Law of Attraction as applying externally. I am pulling something to myself because of a similar vibration, instead of it being a part of my energy field that is not yet perceived in reality.

However, I guess in the end, it does not matter what label we put on these teachings. Do the work and get the benefits, no matter the label.

Ways to Use Clearing Techniques

All the clearing methods can be used independently of an affirmation and visualization program. You do the releasing on the spot for any upsets that happen throughout your day. There is no need to carry anger, jealousy, resentment or other negative emotions around with you.

And, of course, please remember to fill your cleared internal space with love, light and self-approval after clearing.

Another way to approach the clearing methods is to turn your will and your life over to your Higher Power or God instead of using affirmations and visualizations. Then simply use the clearing methods to release negativity.

Or, turn your will and your life over to your Higher Power or Creator; employ the affirmations and visualizations to accomplish what you perceive as God's will and still use the clearing techniques.

It all works! Experiment!

Affirmations for General Well-being

The main focus of *Empower Your Dreams* is to turn specific dreams into reality. But, how about using the same tools in a more general way?

As an example, there is French psychologist Emil Coue's famous statement from over a century ago, "Every day in every way, I am getting better and better." It is such an easy thing to say every day, and I admit that I do just that.

A statement that I often hear in a church I attend is, "Something wonderful is happening to me today!" I like to say this, too, because it sets up a positive expectation for me during the day. I am more inclined to view events as possibly wonderful when I am holding this statement in mind.

Then, there is another general affirmation that I like to make daily. It is, "I have abundant health; I have abundant wealth; I have abundant energy." I have found that it works well to say this affirmation when I am walking because there is a rhythm to it.

My goal is to be as positive and open to opportunities as I can be and these general affirmations help me get in that space. ☀

Chapter Eighteen

My Story

Visualizing and Affirming

Emotional Healing

Energy Healing

Wrapping It Up

Visualizing and Affirming

My story is different from many because I have known about visualizing and affirming since I was about eight years old. That was when my grandmother, Marie, who worked with affirmations, took me to a lecture by Neville Goddard at a Los Angeles Hotel. Neville wrote a number of books on manifesting, including, *Seedtime and Harvest.*

However, when I was a child, I thought like a child, and I don't remember using either potentially life-changing tool until I was eighteen. I turned to visualizing when I was attending college. I was infatuated with someone I had dated a few times and I thought that he was taking too long to telephone me after a date.

I took matters into my own hands, but rather than calling him like you might expect, I imagined hearing my phone ringing and that he was on the line. I did that for a short period of time for two or three days, and then dropped the exercise. There were no results that I could see, as he did not call me during that time.

And, of course, what I did not realize then was that it is not ethical to try to influence someone else's behavior by visualizing. My fellow student had his own free will to decide what he wanted to do with his life. It was not my place to try to influence him to call me by imagining him doing so.

Many years went by and it was in my forties that I really started using the techniques again. I was experiencing health and energy challenges that no doctor I consulted seemed to be able to diagnose. That is when I turned to affirmations, saying that I was in good health and had a lot of energy. Finally, my problem was discovered and I regained robust health again.

A little later, I was experiencing money challenges, and had started working in the Portland area as a real estate sales person. Then, I turned to a small book by Paramahansa Yogananda, called *Scientific Healing Affirmations.* I remember one Sunday when I was holding an open house in a beautiful home, between groups of people walking through, That I would repeat one of Yoganandaji's affirmations for abundance over and over.

And, yes more abundance did eventually come into my life, after many changes and hard work on my part.

Emotional Healing

A few years later, I heard about RET or Rapid Eye Technology. The founder, Ranae Johnson had a school in Salem, Oregon and I went to her for emotional clearing of some painful memories from childhood. The therapy actually worked. I was able to let go of so much. It was hard to believe that watching the tip of a plastic wand move back and forth in front of my eyes could clear emotional trauma. After years of traditional therapy, it did not seem possible, but I experienced the clearing myself.

That was my first experience with a fast way to clear negative emotional states and it felt revolutionary to me. A few years later, I was introduced to tapping, officially known as the Emotional Freedom Technique or EFT. I had an open mind because of my experience with RET, and I found that EFT also worked to clear away negative memories and emotions.

My next experience with clearing techniques happened when I took a workshop based on the teachings of Lester Levenson. This was the first time I focused on creating abundance while clearing away blocking beliefs. I enjoyed the method I learned in the workshop and had a wonderful gift of money came to me immediately after. However, I might have received that gift anyway, because two days prior to the workshop, I went on retreat with the goal of forgiving a family member whom I was resentful of over money.

I was so relieved to finally be able to let my resentment go and get to a place of forgiveness before I left the retreat. Then at the workshop, I worked on letting go of other emotional baggage in regard to abundance and that left me in a very clear energy place. It was the day after the workshop that I unexpectedly received, what was to me, a quite large gift from that family member.

In 2006 when I was over 50 years old, I ran for my first public office. It was for a nonpartisan seat on my local water board. I did indeed beat the incumbent and win in the November election! What stands out for me in the election campaign as far as energy work goes, is that I had to release some heavy duty anxiety about serving as an elected official before I could see myself winning. I did the letting go and then I could campaign effectively.

Since then, I have continued to work with a variety of clearing techniques, pairing them with visualizations and a system of affirmations spelled out in the decks of the Little Cards.

Energy Healing

I have worked with prayer and energy healing all of my life. I was raised as a Christian Scientist where it was expected that you would heal yourself of physical ailments with prayer. My family also went to doctors, but the first choice for me was always to try prayer. As a teenager, I broadened my studies to include a variety of New Thought Teachings and continued on that path until I discovered the writings of Paramahansa Yogananda. I now consider myself a yogi and follow Yoganandaji's teachings.

In 1989 I was initiated into the first degree of Usui Reiki from a distinguished lineage. My Reiki Master was initiated by Grand Master Phyllis Furumoto of the Reiki Alliance. Furumoto was the granddaughter of Hawayo Takata who brought Reiki to the West from Japan and Takata Sensei chose Furumoto to carry on her work after her passing, which occurred in 1980.

I received my second degree initiation in 1990 and then practiced in Friday Harbor on San Juan Island in Washington state while I lived there. Reiki is such a beneficial healing energy! I continue to use it almost daily.

Wrapping Up

I have shared my story with you to show that I have believed that an unseen energy powers our Universe ever since I can remember. I personally call that energy God and believe that we can work with that energy to heal and create what we desire. These teachings are part of that belief.

And I am happy to say that my life is good today. I am clearer now than I have ever been, thanks to this work and probably the meditation I do as well. Not everything has come to me yet that I am working on, but I have faith that it will, if it is for my highest good. In the meantime, life flows so much more smoothly and good things continue to happen.

In closing, I believe that we are in an amazing place in time right now, with so much knowledge available to us that used to be hidden. What is written about in *Empower Your Dreams* is a part of this knowledge. Now it is up to us to find what works for ourselves, have faith, and go for the good.

I wish you all the best on your continued life journey... ☀

Thank you

Thanks to Christiann Klein for being there to discuss with me the message in *Empower Your Dreams* and how to present it. I appreciate my friends Reverand Mary Jane Lavendier Shea and Peter Shea for reading the manuscript and pointing out areas that needed clarification. I am thankful to my granddaughter Alexa for thoroughly proof reading the manuscript and my friend Gerry Mitchell for proof reading and raising grammar questions to be addressed. My gratitude also goes to my friend and book designer Susan Wells for her eye-catching cover design and book format.

Thank you all! I could not have produced *Empower Your Dreams* in the form that it is without you. ☀

About the Author

Janna Lee is the pen name of the author. *Empower Your Dreams* is her second book and her first self-help, inspirational one. She lives in Southern California.

Janna serves as an elected local official in her community and has done so for fourteen years. She ran for this, her first elected office, when she was over 50 years old. She wrote, published and successfully marketed her first book when she was over 60. Janna says, "I believe that the tools in this book can help you to achieve anything you want to achieve, no matter your age."

You can buy the *Empower Your Dreams* paperback online at Amazon or eBay and the Kindle e-book on Amazon. The decks of Little Cards on various affirmation topics are also available on eBay under the search names, "Little Cards," or "Affirmation Cards."

For more information about in-person or online workshops, go to Janna's Facebook page, Janna Lee, Author. She also invites you to follow her on Twitter **@JannaAuthor**. To contact Janna, email: **EmpowerDreams22@gmail.com**.

Janna Lee wishes you a Happy Journey. ☀

Made in United States
North Haven, CT
14 July 2022

21340432R00074